e f g

l m n o p

w x y z

Written and illustrated by Loris Lesynski

Annick Press

Toronto • New York • Vancouver

© 2004 Loris Lesynski (text and illustrations)
Second Printing, July 2005

Annick Press Ltd.
All rights reserved. No part of this work covered by the copyrights hereon may be reproduced or used in any form or by any means—graphic, electronic, or mechanical—without the prior written permission of the publisher.

We acknowledge the support of the Canada Council for the Arts, the Ontario Arts Council, and the Government of Canada through the Book Publishing Industry Development Program (BPIDP) for our publishing activities.

Cataloging in Publication Data

Lesynski, Loris
    Zigzag : zoems for zindergarten / written and illustrated by Loris Lesynski.

Poems.
ISBN 1-55037-875-9 (bound)
ISBN 1-55037-882-1 (pbk.)

1. Children's poetry, Canadian (English). I. Title.
PS8573.E79Z457 2004   jC811'.54   C2004-902072-2

Distributed in Canada by:
Firefly Books Ltd.
66 Leek Crescent
Richmond Hill, ON L4B 1H1

Published in the U.S.A. by:
Annick Press (U.S.) Ltd.

Distributed in the U.S.A. by:
Firefly Books (U.S.) Inc.
P.O. Box 1338
Ellicott Station
Buffalo, NY 14205

Printed and bound in Canada by Friesens, Altona, Manitoba.

The illustrations in this book were done in watercolor, colored pencil, and gouache. The text was typeset in Utopia, the titles in Lemonade.

Write to Loris Lesynski at
Annick Press, 15 Patricia Ave., Toronto, Ontario, Canada M2M 1H9

www.lorislesynski.com

www.annickpress.com

ZIGZAG

Kindergarten Rocks!

Big kids, little kids,

girls and boys,

books and paints

and games and toys

    —kindergarten rocks!

Colorful mats, unusual hats.

Puppets, puzzles, balls and bats.

Numbers, letters—all of that's

    —why kindergarten rocks!

Zigzag

zigzag here and zigzag there
see some zigzags everywhere

zigzag edges on a paper bag

fences go in a zig and zag

zigzag notches on a front door key

the zigzag shape of a Christmas tree

zigzag string on a basketball hoop

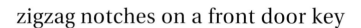

see some zigzag noodles in my soup!

zigzag red and yellow stripes on a clown

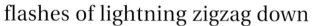

flashes of lightning zigzag down

snowflakes zigzag as they fall

... and what about the bounce

what about the bounce

what about the bounce of a Ping Pong ball?

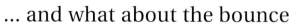

Imagine

some **bananas** in a zigzag bunch

or zigzag **sandwiches** just for lunch

zigzag **eyebrows**?

crayons, too

zigzag **stripes** on the zebra at the zoo

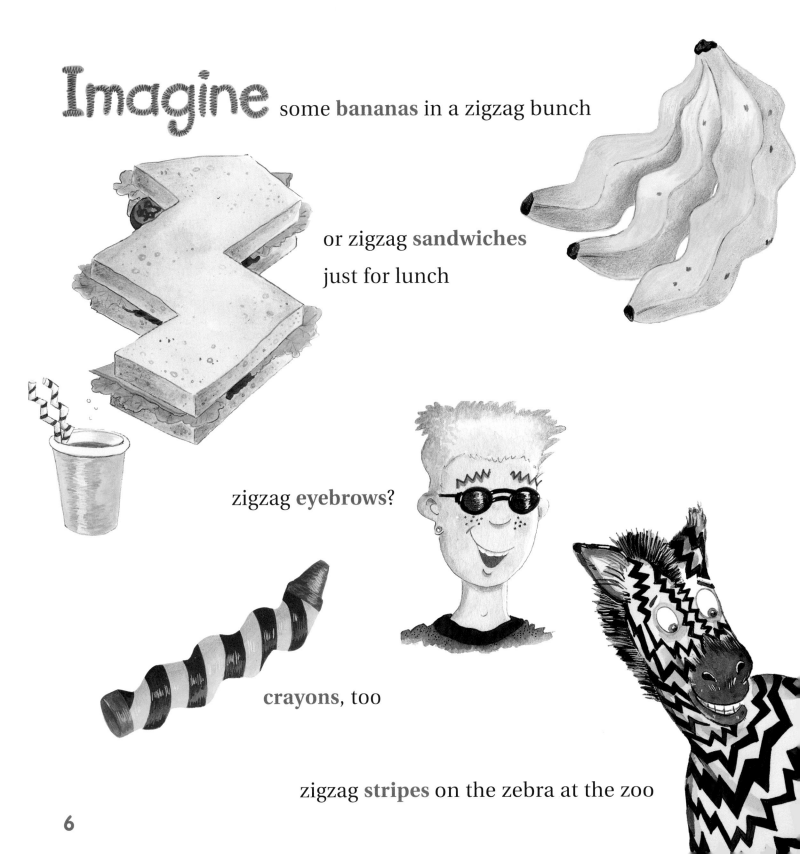

Up-and-down shoulders

back-and-forth feet

get your body going in a **zigga zagga** beat

zigzag elbows

zigzag toes

zigzag thumbs

... and a ziggy zaggy, wiggle waggle,

jiggle jaggy **nose**

Sit on Your Bottom

not on your elbows

not on your knees

sit on your bottom

please please please

not on your head

not upside down

sit on your bottom

and turn around

not on your nose

not on your chin

sit on your bottom

and let's begin

TA DA!

8

Lap

Where's my lap?

Where'd it go?

It was here a minute ago.

I know!

I
STOOD
UP!

Here's my lap,
back again.
It seemed to disappear and then

I
SAT
DOWN!

thumb thumb
finger fingers
palm palm CLAP
let your fingers hug
and have a cuddle
in your lap

Anything's a Drum

anything's a drum drum

a can can be a drum drum

tabletop's a drum drum

chair a double chum drum

drum drum anywhere, drum drum in the air

knees can be a drum drum
both of them a fun drum
hands are for a clap-drum
floor is for a tap-drum

drum drum anywhere, drum drum in the air

elbows-touch-each-other drum
head can be another drum
drumming in the air drum
drumming anywhere

drum drum anywhere

drum drum in the air, drum drum anywhere

drum

drum

drum

Hamster Rock 'n' Roll

The kindergarten hamster, round and round he goes,
running faster, faster on his little hamster toes.

Having fun, he loves to run in such a busy way.
But is he ever dizzy at the end of the day?

Paintbrush

paintbrush paintbrush

I love how you sway

I'd like to paint and paint all day

paintbrush paintbrush

I love how you swirl

together today

we'll paint the world

paintbrush paintbrush

tomorrow we'll play

it's time to wash you and

put you away

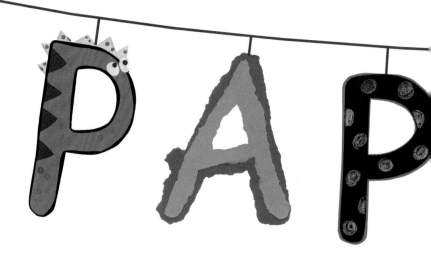

paper to paint on

paper to read

paper for presents

paper you need

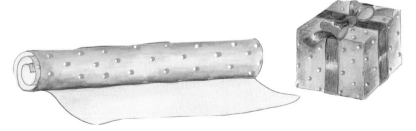

14

paper is flat, but glue and tape
can make it into any shape

if I were made of paper
and you were paper too,
we'd go to school in an envelope
and close the door with glue

15

Scissors

my scissors never listen

when I tell them what to cut

I try to cut a circle out of yellow paper but

    it

        looks

            like

               this:

my scissors never listen

when I try to cut a square

it comes out kind of crooked

looking something like a bear

      like

        this:

click clack, cut it slow
snip snip, cut it straight
slow down, go around
cut cut, concentrate

THEN
my scissors listen
tell 'em "Open"
tell 'em "Shut"
I practice how to use them
and I practice how to cut
now I'm cutting circles
now I'm cutting squares
now I'm zigzag cutting out
a row of perfect stairs
like this!

17

Stomp Up Steps

Stomp up steps
  stomp back down
    one stomp sideways
      one stomp around.

Sway up steps
  sway back down
    one sway sideways
      one sway around.

Tiptoe up
  tiptoe down
    one tip sideways
      one toe around.

S l o w up steps
  s l o w back down
    s l o w l y sideways
      s l o w l y around.

18

Zero

zero is nothing

zero is none

zero's not any

zero's no fun

a **zillion** is oodles

a zillion's a lot

a zillion is many

so many, too many

a zillion is probably more

than we've got

Monkeys on Monday

We're ...

monkeys on Monday,

toads on Tuesday,

wiggle worms on Wednesday, round then flat.

Birds on Thursday.

Elephants Friday.

The teacher says we're just like that,

like that.

The Alphabet

the alphabet has A in it

and X in it and K in it

it's why we like to play in it

and know just how it goes

letters, letters

everywhere,

in books, on T-shirts, underwear

the little bits of alphabet

together dance and then we get

a story ✔

a poem ✔

a joke ✔

a song ✔

a million zillion ways in which the letters all belong

Mrs. Zebra

Our teacher

Mrs. Zebra

likes

stripes

we try to find them

all the time

stripes

stripes on T-shirts

stripes on socks

stripes on books and

trucks and blocks

stripes we paint

stripes we draw

news of special stripes

we saw

stripes!

Zack Had a Cat

Zack had a cat
and the cat was white.
It whirled and twirled in the morning light.

Zack had a cat
and the cat was pink.
It sailed all day in the kitchen sink.

Zack had a cat
and the cat was black.
It liked to hide in his plaid backpack.

Zack had a cat
and the cat was red.
It named itself Tomato Head.

Zack had a cat that he painted blue,
then he made a mouse of playdough, too.

Oh, yes!

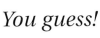

Zack had a cat as
yellow as the sun.
Which of the cats was
the favorite one?

You guess!

TEE HEE HEE

TEE HEE HEE
and *ha ha ha*
boo hoo hoo
and *lala lala* LA.
Whoopee!
Yippee!
Vroom vroom vroom!
School is over,
leave the room.
    Yak yak yak
    and sing and shout.
    Time to let the noises out!

Cars Coming?

Kids are fast
but cars are faster.
    Look both ways or else disaster.
Kids are big
but trucks are jumbo.
    Running out is strictly dumbo.
Kids are cute
but wheels don't care.
    Check the traffic, see what's there.

Gumbo Baloney

Gumbo Baloney is the dog down the street.

Two sharp ears and four big feet.

Wet nose, one, and black spots, three.

I'd like him more if I didn't see

  so many

    so many

      so many
        TEETH.

What is mud? I do not know.
Where's it come from? Does it grow?
Mud is what it is, and so
all it is is
MUD.

A little earth, a little rain,
mixed together. What's its name?
MUD.

The garden when it's very wet,
and has no grass or flowers yet—
MUD.

The bottom of a puddle when
you jump right in and out again—
MUD.

Orange Popsicles...

Orange Popsicles, pink lemonade
    cupcake sprinkles in every shade
chocolate icing, cherry Jell-O
    beans of green and corn of yellow
the bread was white
    with blueberry jam
makes me wonder
    what color I am
                        ... inside

Kitchen

Reeeeeeeeeeee ...

> friger-iger-igerator
> keep it cold
> I'll have it later

> stove! *hot!* stove! *hot!*
> boil potatoes in a pot
> (want to touch it? better not!)
> *hot* stove! stove *hot!*

> soup cans, frying pans
> cupboards full of food
> sitting in the kitchen puts us
> in a hungry mood

peanut butter, jam and honey, fill a spoon for me
after school the kitchen is the **nicest** place to be

Kindergarten Raps

Kindergarten

bindergarten

peppergarten

salt

smartygarten

partygarten

millymarten

malt

Follow me, wallow me, wallaby woe

follow me, mollow me

somebody's slow

hurry up giddy-up

get up and go

somebody's faster—*it's me!*

ABCD

HIJK

QRSTUV